Change For Children

Authors

Sandra Nina Kaplan
Jo Ann Butom Kaplan
Sheila Kunishima Madsen
Bette K. Taylor

Goodyear Publishing Company, Inc.
Pacific Palisades, California

Change For Children

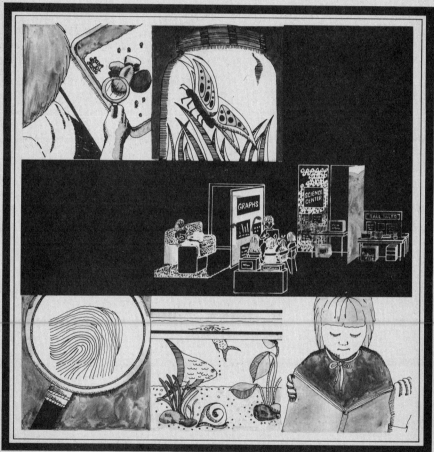

Ideas and Activities for Individualizing Learning

Copyright © 1973
GOODYEAR PUBLISHING COMPANY, INC.
Pacific Palisades, California

Current printing (last digit):
10 9 8 7 6 5 4 3
ISBN: 0-87620-145-1

Library of Congress Catalog
Card Number: 72-94423

Y-1451-7

Printed in the United States of America

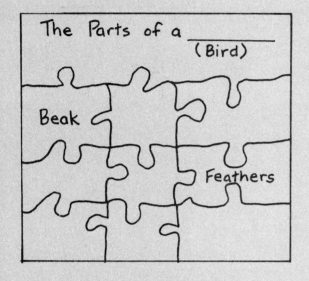

The Parts of a _____
(Bird)

Beak

Feathers

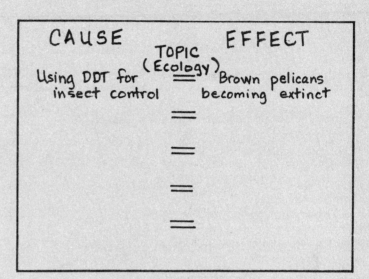

CAUSE   EFFECT
TOPIC
(Ecology)
Using DDT for   Brown pelicans
insect control   becoming extinct

COMPARE

	From study (Heart)	Outside study (Engine)
DIFFERENT		
ALIKE		

Choose one thing from your study.
Compare it to something outside your study.

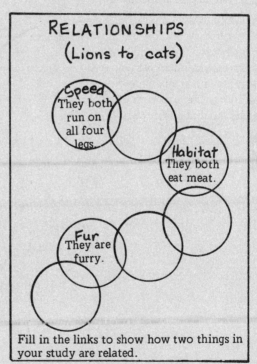

RELATIONSHIPS
(Lions to cats)

Speed
They both run on all four legs.

Habitat
They both eat meat.

Fur
They are furry.

Fill in the links to show how two things in your study are related.

TEACHER INTERVENTION

Why the Teacher Intervenes

Student-teacher interaction is necessary during independent study. The interaction may be a formally structured conference or a casual conversation as the teacher circulates around the room while the students are working. The teacher intervenes with the student in order to:

> keep in touch
> help with problem-solving
> provide direction
> open up new areas for exploration and production
> give encouragement
> introduce, teach, and/or reinforce a needed skill

Some Questions to be Asked When Intervening

> Do you have enough materials?
> What do you need?
> Are you having trouble finding information?
> Do you need help in reading any of the material?
> Do you understand the information?
> Can you find the information you need in order to answer your question(s)?
> How much longer do you think it will take to finish this part of the study?

MAKING PROJECTS FROM RAW MATERIALS

Creative independent study products result when students are allowed to select and manipulate raw materials. Collecting and placing raw materials in a specific location within the room acts as a stimulus for possible independent study products. Students should be encouraged to mix and match materials and use the materials in new and different ways.

Project Cubes

Project cubes are a method of sharing and categorizing processed information and a way to motivate others toward independent study.

Boxes of all shapes and sizes can be used to show the parts of a particular study.

Within one box the student can depict on six sides: subtopics, answers to questions, or concepts learned. With many boxes the student can build a pyramid to illustrate the varying aspects of his study.

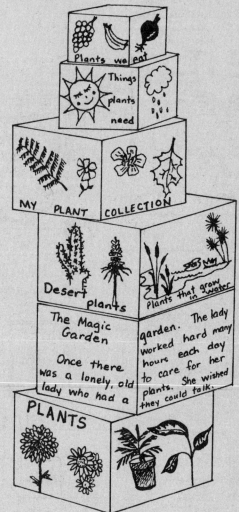

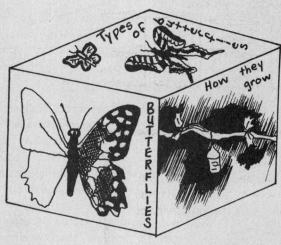

Mobile

Some aspect or concept of the student's independent study can be creatively structured into a mobile art form.

Cans

Each can indicates a sub-area, question, or phase of the student's independent study and becomes a compartment for facts, pictures, and items within that category.

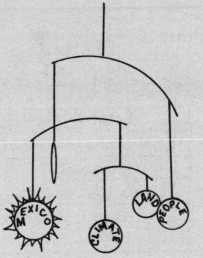

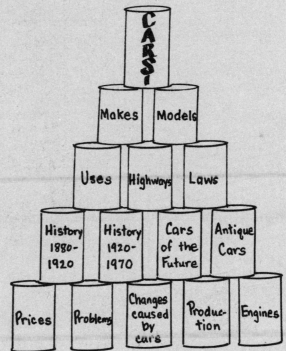

How the information is converted into an independent study product is dependent on the student's artistic interests, the alternatives the teacher has presented, and the availability of raw materials.

Venetian Blinds

Questions and answers from the student's independent study can be exhibited on venetian blinds: questions on one side, answers on the other. Rules can be created which allow other children to use this product as a question/answer game.

Museum

Formed from a box, the museum houses the personal treasures the student has collected or made in relationship to the topic he has studied.

Sculpture

An area or concept of the student's independent study can be symbolized or developed in an abstract form by using scrap materials.

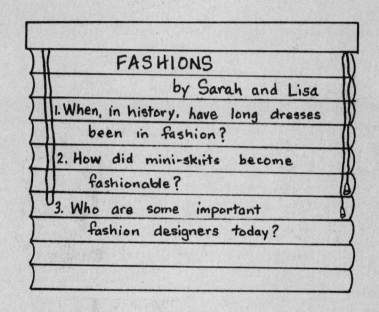

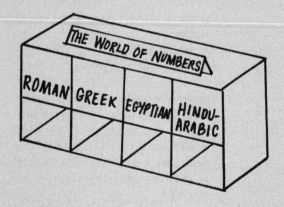

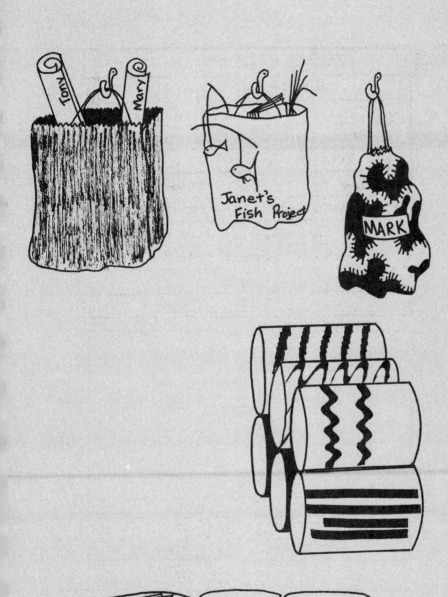

STORING PROJECTS

While students engage in independent study, the amount and types of products in progress can become cumbersome. Storage containers can be created which save space while still making the projects ac-

Sacks

A collection of all types of shopping bags can become storage containers. Hung on hooks, knobs, backs of chairs, coat racks, or hangers, these receptacles are transportable and conveniently kept so that students can easily store their independent study materials.

Ice Cream Containers

Five gallon ice cream containers can be used to store independent study projects. These containers can be stacked to form a set of cubicles by punching holes through them and then securing them with string, yarn, or wire. They can also be stacked separately so that children can pick them up and take them to the area where they will work. Materials needed for the study (books, notes, paper, etc.), as well as the project in progress, can be kept within the container.

RECORD KEEPING

The purpose of independent study record-keeping devices is to encourage student responsibility while keeping the teacher apprised of what the student has been doing.

Contract

Contracts such as these provide a teacher-student agreement within a given time limit.

The expectations for the study are clearly defined by the student with the assistance of the teacher. The contract represents a commitment for a course of action.

Log

This log assists the student in planning and following through on his independent study. It also may serve to help the student evaluate his progress.

~CONTRACT~

_____ with _____
(Student)   (teacher)

SUBJECT: _____

CONTRACTUAL CONDITIONS

What I want to find out:	How I will show what I learned:

DUE DATE: _____
CONSEQUENCES: _____

NAME: _____ DUE DATE: _____

Planning Date: _____

Subject of my study: _____

What I want to find out: _____

_____

Evaluation: _____

Signed: _____
        (student)   (teacher)

KEEPING TRACK OF MY INDEPENDENT STUDY

LOG OF MY INDEPENDENT STUDY			
Date	Accomplishments	Evaluation	Next step- (Plans)

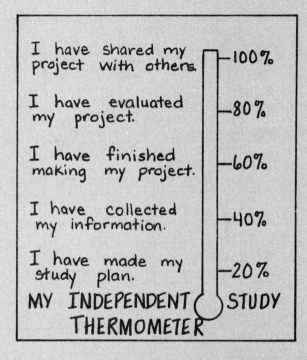

Individual Thermometer

Each student records the progress of his independent study as he moves through the various activities listed on the thermometer.

Group Thermometer

The five thermometers on the bulletin board indicate major activities each student is expected to complete. As a student finishes the activity, he computes the class percentage on the corresponding thermometer.

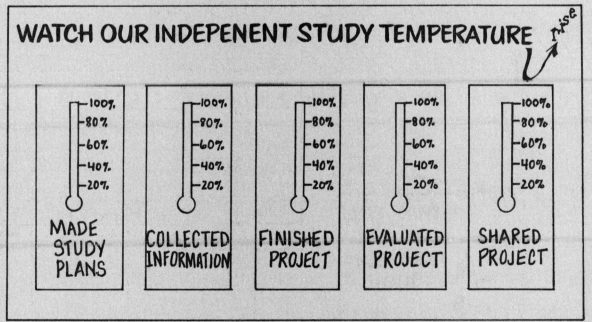

Group Ladder

Each rung of the ladder indicates an activity the learner must do in sequence as part of the independent study program. The student moves his marker as he completes each step of the independent study program.

Individual Ladder

One bulletin board can be set aside for independent study record keeping. Each student's ladder represents an outline of the student's study plan as well as his progress in completing the plan.

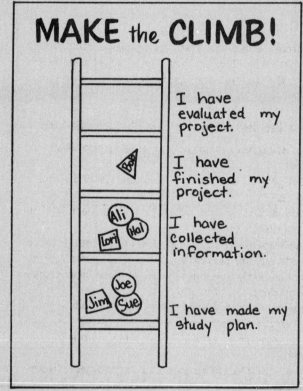

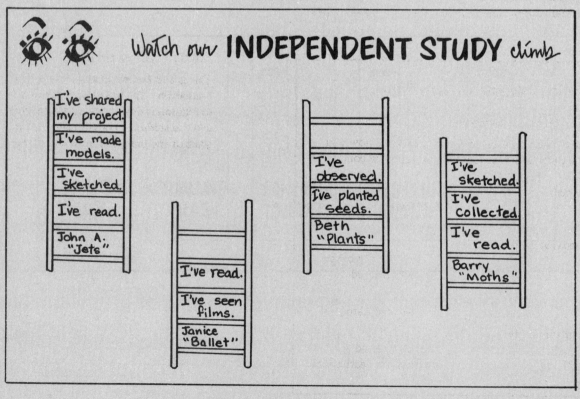

EVALUATIONS

Teacher-Student Conferences

Teacher-student conferences are scheduled or informal meetings where the student shows what he has done and explains why he has done it. Emphasis is placed on the student's learning to evaluate his own independent study project.

Key Questions the Teacher Might Discuss With the Student

What do you like best about the project you are doing (or have completed)? Why?

What parts of your project caused you difficulties? How did you solve these problems?

What new skills did you learn while working on the project (such as typing, lettering, outlining, etc.)?

What sources of information did you use? Did all the sources agree?

Was your independent study plan reasonable as far as goals and time allotment were concerned? How might your plan have been changed? How could other students use your project?

How did you collect or keep track of your information while you were studying? Can you think of another method to use?

What new ideas for another study did you get from the one you have just finished?

Do you have any unanswered questions about your subject? How might you find the answers?

How could you challenge or interest others to study your subject?

Student Self-Evaluation

This is a self-administered, subjective evaluation. The instrument for this evaluation is developed by the teacher and the student in relationship to the goals of the independent study plan.

Example: Independent Study Profile

Name _____ Subject _____ Date _____

Directions: Place a check on each continuum to show how you feel about the independent study you have completed.

1. Use of Resources
   many _____ few
   same _____ different

2. Finished Project (or Product)
   ordinary _____ unlike any others
   written _____ constructed

3. Use of Time
   wasted _____ worked hard

4. Feelings About the Study
   satisfied _____ dissatisfied
   learned enough _____ need to learn more

Class Sharing

The student is given an opportunity to orally present the end-product of his independent study to the class. Class members respond with questions and/or comments which may clarify or challenge the student's learnings. "The Key Questions the Teacher Might Discuss With the Student," as listed under *Teacher-Student Conferences*, might also be used in this situation. The group should develop standards which serve as a reference as they share and discuss their independent studies.

Independent Study Committee

This committee is made up of from six to eight classmates chosen by the students and the teacher. The standards for evaluation and discussion of the student's independent study are developed by the group. The evaluation of the independent study is a composite of the group's reaction to it.

Example of Committee Standards for Independent Study Evaluation

Did the student try to use many sources for his information?
Did he conference with the teacher when he needed help?
Did he try to share his information in new and unusual ways?
Was he able to summarize what he learned?

Planning Classroom Time
5

GETTING THE STUDENT INTO MOTION

Planning devices may help students to determine:

WHAT? the activity they select from the alternatives available to them

WHEN? the sequence of the activities they will do within a period or block of time

HOW? the means they will use to perform the activities they have chosen

WHERE? the place they will work

Any or all of these points may be incorporated into a planning device.

The purpose of any planning device is to provide the student with a tool that will help him become an independent and responsible learner and increase his awareness of his abilities and interests. The use of any planning device should enable the student to develop a self-directedness which can be applied in and out of the classroom.

Planning devices provide students with formats that assist them in budgeting their time, programming their learnings, and making decisions from the choice of activities available to them. The type of schedule used depends on the teacher's intent and the students' needs and capabilities. All of the devices offer students a range of choices.

Rotational Scheduling

Groups of children are rotated to learning activities. In this type of scheduling, students do not decide when they will go to the activity or center, but rather what they will do when they get to that activity or center.

Assignments

Children are assigned to activities or centers according to diagnosed needs. They may choose *when* to go to the assigned area and/or *what* to do at the assigned area.

Contracting

Students develop an agreement which states their choices of what to do, when to do it, and how to do it.

Self-programming

Students are given freedom to set their own course of learning from those activities available in the environment. The teacher may initially allow only the independent students to program themselves while she works with others who are more dependent on teacher direction. The students may move from programming themselves for a small portion of each day to programming themselves for the entire day. The goal is for each student to find his own way to best use his time.

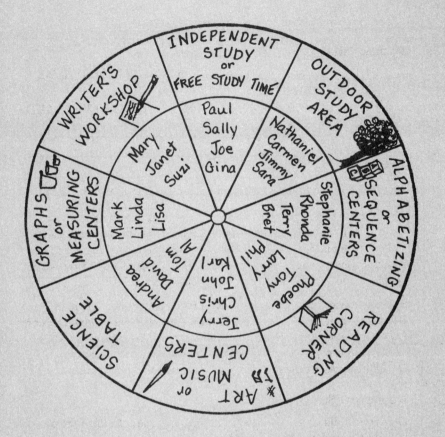

THE STUDENT'S DAY

Circle Planning

The experiences which the teacher thinks are imperative for students are written on the outer circle. The teacher controls the sequence of places where students work by rotating the inner circle during the day, or she can change it at the beginning of each day and instruct the students to do each activity by moving clockwise.

Trail Planning

Each trail represents a sequence of learning activities. Students can be assigned to a trail, or they can select one. This method of planning assures that all students will work at all the areas.

Postcard

The teacher and students can design their own postcards. These act as personalized communications between the teacher and the student. They inform the student of the tasks that have been assigned to him. The student returns the postcards to relate his accomplishments.

Cut and Past Schedule

Assignments for the total class are written in some of the geometric shapes on the ditto by the teacher. The extra shapes are filled in by the teacher and/or student for individualized assignments. When the student completes an assignment, he cuts out the shape on which the assignment was written and pastes it on the other side of the ditto.

Oct. 6

Dear *Sally*
A reminder to:

- Finish your Insect Collection
- Do 3 graphs
- Practice capital letters in cursive writing
- Do 2 activities from the Tall Tales Center
- Help Joan with her multiplication work

Mrs. S.

Return to sender by: Oct. 14

Mrs. S: I have...

CUT AND PASTE AS YOU FINISH YOUR WORK

CUT HERE

THINGS I'VE DONE

PASTE HERE

Visit Writer's Workshop

Do 3 measuring activities

Read a library book Do a book sharing activity.

Contract Date: _____

§ I agree to complete the
following work by _____
                         (Date)

_____

_____

_____

Room 2 Official Seal

_____

_____

_____

Student's
Signature

Teacher's
Signature

Paul W.	MY PLANS				
	MONDAY	TUESDAY	WEDNESDAY	THURSDAY	FRIDAY
Opening / Planning time					
9:15-9:45	ASSEMBLY			Film	
9:45-10:15	ASSEMBLY				
10:15	RECESS				
10:30-11:30		Visit Library		Neighborhood Walk	
11:30	LUNCH				
12:30-1:30	Animal Stories Group	Tall Tales Group	Animal Stories Group	Tall Tales Group	
1:30	PHYSICAL EDUCATION				
2:00-2:30					Film
2:30	EVALUATION / CLEAN-UP				
Schedule O.K'd	_____ student initials _____ teacher initials				

Learning Contract

Students contract with the teacher to get involved in a learning experience or to perform a specific task. This contract should be developed cooperatively and the terms must be clearly understood by the student. Before signing the contract, he must know the time allotted to complete the work and the consequences if he fails to fulfill the contract.

My Plans

The plans made for the total class are dittoed. The open time blocks are filled in by the student. The schedule is considered to be a contractual agreement when it is initialed by both the teacher and the student. The student's initials signify his commitment to fulfill his plans. The teacher's initials signify her approval of the student's program.

Floor Plan

A diagram or model of the classroom is made. Each student places his flag on the area where he has chosen to work. This method of planning presents the students with an overview of all the learning possibilities which are available to them within the room. It also aids the teacher in keeping track of where students are working at a given time. The diagram can be charted and placed on a bulletin board, or it can be outlined with paint or masking tape on the classroom floor.

Must Planning

The teacher can control learning by presenting students with certain requirements for which they are responsible. Students write their own plans around the outside of the "musts." Each student is expected to schedule his time to include the "musts." But the student decides when to do them.

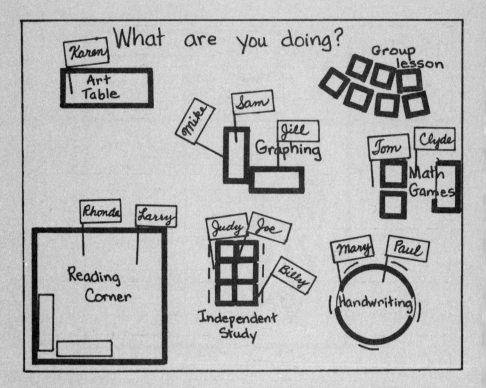

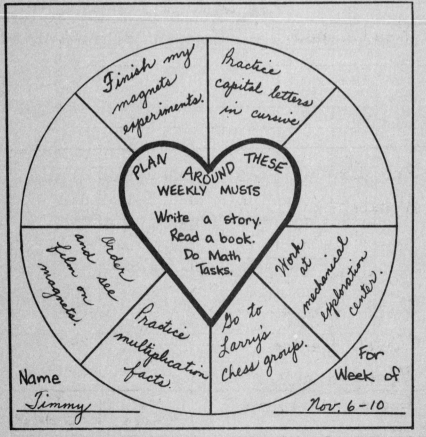

My Plans Name_____	
Write a book	
Games	
Project	
Records, tapes	
Filmstrips	
Flashcards be w see	
Read a book	

My Plans

Children select and number the activities in the order they will do them. Planning sheets which use pictures help primary students to make learning choices.

Planning Checklist

This planning sheet is designed to schedule children for a particular subject area and block of time. Listed are the learning choices for an individualized language arts program. The student checks where he is going to work. After completing the activity, the student places an **X** alongside of his choice.

	My Choice	I Completed
Art Center		
Alphabetizing Center		
Animal Center		
Go to the Library		
Read a book		
Vowel Center		
Write a story		
I can plan by myself. Name:		

THE TEACHER'S DAY

Who needs my help?

What skills or subjects need to be taught?

What must I do to motivate interest in a center or subject?

The teacher's answers to these questions will determine how he structures his day, interacting with groups and individuals. His daily routine must allow time for teaching, and for engaging in dialogue and intervention with students. For efficient planning and scheduling the teacher must competently assess the class needs and assign priorities for his time on the basis of these needs.

The teacher's schedule should always be a flexible outline of activities. Leaving empty blocks of time allows the teacher freedom to work with students as their needs arise.

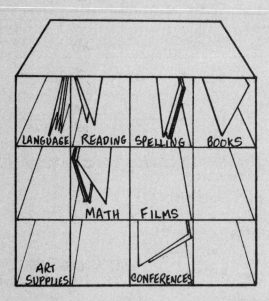

TIME ZONES	TODAY Jan. 5
9:30 – 10:00	Math: Addition of fractions — Mary, Sammy, Tom, Janet
10:00 – 10:30	Individual Conferences 1. Jane 2. Larry 3. Bob 4. Lynne
10:30 – 10:45	Give out materials children requested

LANGUAGE · READING · SPELLING · BOOKS

MATH · FILMS

ART SUPPLIES · CONFERENCES

Name Mark L.
Date Jan. 4
I need: some clay to make a model for my project.

Chart Planning

A teacher may use a large spiral tablet to communicate with students, informing the class of what will be done at various times during the school day. This method allows the teacher flexibility in planning each day according to the students changing needs.

Slot Planning

Students record their needs and interests on cards. These cards are placed into slots which have been labeled for different subject or activity areas. The teacher surveys the cards at the end of each day or week and uses them as a reference in planning time and activities for the class.

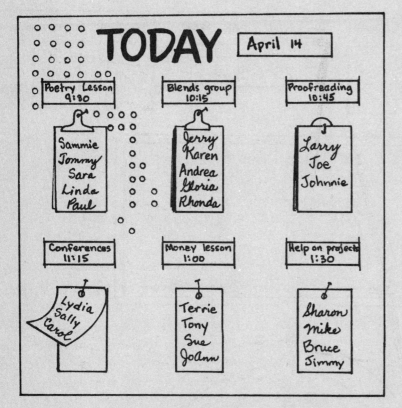

Today

Pads of paper clipped or hooked onto pieces of wood or cardboard form charts which can be used to announce the teacher's schedule for the day. Activity and time headings are written on slips of paper which are slipped into pre-cut slots above each pad. Students sign up for the activities on the pads of paper.

Chalkboard

The teacher fills in the chalkboard outline with the class at the beginning of the school day. This type of planning is a quick and efficient method of indicating what the teacher has planned for certain students. It is also a way of communicating the learning possibilities available to the class.

MRS. B's PLANS - TUESDAY

GRAPHS CENTER - 9:30
Tony, Mary, Paul,
John, Trina

TELLING TIME
LESSON - 10:00
  at the carpet
anyone interested

INDIVIDUAL CONFERENCES - at my desk - 10:30 - 11:30
1. Paul (bring Math work)   5.
2. Linda (bring Story folder)   6.
3. Lisa (make out a new   7.
     behavior agreement)
4. Terri (bring Library book)   8.

SYLLABLES GROUP   WATERCOLOR LESSON
  1:00 at the carpet   2:00 at the Art Table
Jerry, Sally, Tim, Mike   1.   4.
                                  2.   5.
                                  3.   6.

PLANNING FOR WORK OUTSIDE THE CLASSROOM AND SPECIAL EVENTS

Cup Hook Rack

A rack made of cup hooks inserted into a piece of lumber can be used to keep track of students who are working in areas outside the classroom. Students hang their name cards below the label of the place where they can be found.

Chalkboard

A small chalkboard is placed near a classroom door. Children sign out before leaving the room by writing their names and the areas to which they are going.

Clock Out

Each student is expected to record his name and the place where he will be working on a slip of paper. This is placed in the chart opposite the time he is leaving the room.

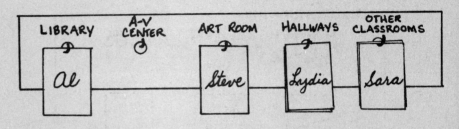

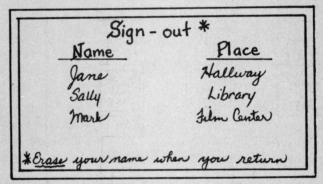

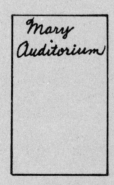

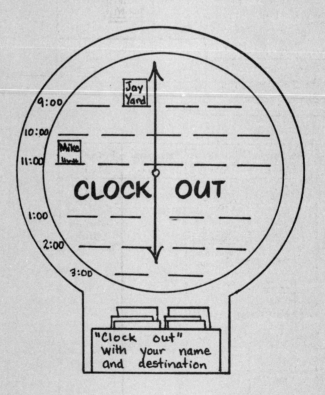

Special Happenings

Advertising special events is a means of introducing and motivating students to current happenings available to them. A sign is clipped over a pocket to announce the activity being presented. The students who wish to participate in the event sign up on strips of paper which they place in the correctly labeled pocket on the chart. This process stimulates student involvement and commitment for the activity. The number of students who can be part of the event can also be regulated.

Acetate Overlay

The use of acetate or plastic over a master weekly schedule enables the teacher to reuse the chart each week. With crayon or grease pencil, the special events for the week are recorded for the students.

Monday May 1	Tuesday May 2	Wednesday May 3	Thursday May 4	Friday May 5
9:30 -Sewing		9:30 -Sewing		9:30 -Sewing
10:00 -African Slides		10:00 -African Slides		- Rhythm Band
- Bird Walk	11:00 Map Making			

Record Keeping
6

THE IMPORTANCE OF RECORD KEEPING

PARENT: "How is Tommy's schoolwork?"
STUDENT: "What have I been learning?"
TEACHER: "How will I know what each child is doing?"
PRINCIPAL: "Mr. Jones, how are you accounting for your students'
            learning?"

Record keeping is a continuous process which involves the student and the teacher in accounting and reporting individual growth and learning progress. The devices used for record keeping indicate which tasks the student has undertaken and how much he has accomplished. While records show what the student has done, they also help in planning for future learnings.

The teacher and the student share the responsibilities for maintaining the records. They also decide which record-keeping instruments and procedures to employ.

Record keeping cannot be separated from evaluation. Whereas record keeping tells what has been accomplished, evaluation tells how well it has been accomplished.

For the Parent: Records form a comprehensive picture of the student's activities in the classroom.

For the Student: Record keeping develops the child's responsibility for charting and following through on a course of study. It provides the child with a feeling of accomplishment and an identity as a learner. The record-keeping process also helps students to see many possibilities for learning.

For the Teacher: Records supply the teacher with a permanent accounting of what the student has been doing, and thus allows the teacher to further plan and provide for the student. Records are a reference for interpreting pupil progress to parents.

RECORD KEEPING FOR CONFERENCES

Anecdotal Records Notebook

This notebook can be used by the teacher for recording information gathered in conferences and from observations. Records can be used to plan skill groups, report to parents, and show ongoing progress during the year.

Conference Record

This is a method of recording each child's conferences with the teacher throughout the year. Any code may be developed to meet a teacher's needs. The circled letters indicate conferences that have already been held. The empty circles indicate conferences the teacher or child plan to have. At a glance, the teacher can see children she has not conferenced with recently. The record sheet can act as a reminder for writing anecdotal records at the end of the day or week.

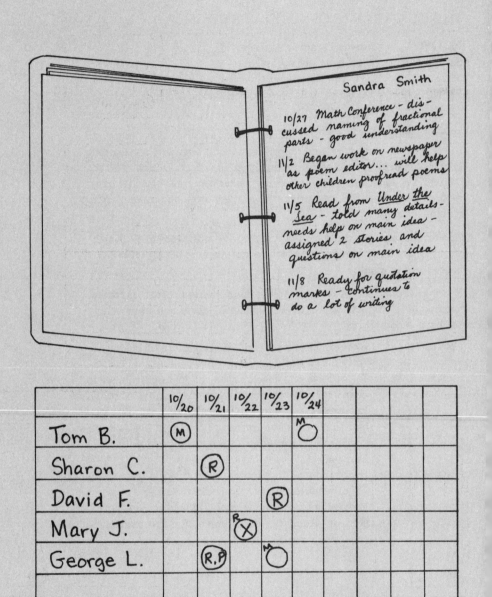

Sandra Smith

10/27 Math Conference - discussed naming of fractional parts - good understanding

11/2 Began work on newspaper as poem editor... will help other children proofread poems

11/5 Read from Under the Sea - told many details - needs help on main idea - assigned 2 stories and questions on main idea

11/8 Ready for quotation marks - continues to do a lot of writing

	10/20	10/21	10/22	10/23	10/24			
Tom B.	Ⓜ				ᴹ◯			
Sharon C.		Ⓡ						
David F.				Ⓡ				
Mary J.			Ⓡ⊗					
George L.		Ⓡ,Ⓟ		ᴹ◯				

Ⓜ = Math Conference held

Ⓟ = Proofreading Conference held

Ⓡ = Reading Conference held

ᴹ◯ = indicates Math Conference is needed
circle is "X'd" when Conference is completed

WHAT HAVE YOU READ?

Date Started	Title of Book	Author	Date Finished	Comments

MY LIBRARY

TITLE:
AUTHOR:

RECORD KEEPING FOR READING

My Library and
What Have You Read?

Either page may be used by individual children as a personal reading record. These records may be kept in a notebook, a file box, or a pocket chart at the reading center, or each child may keep his own sheet or card in his reading or work folder. These pages provide a basis of information to help the teacher schedule small group instruction according to needs and interests.

Reading Circles

The teacher identifies the skill areas the students will learn and the activities they will do. Coloring over a part of each circle indicates what the student has accomplished.

Record Garden

A paper cup, a pipe cleaner and colored paper are used to construct the garden. The skill the student is working on is printed on a piece of paper which becomes the center for a flower. The activities which the student has done to learn the skill are written on paper also. These become petals for the flower, and they are glued to the pipe cleaner stem. Students can make a different garden for each skill they are learning, or they can add another flower to the same garden.

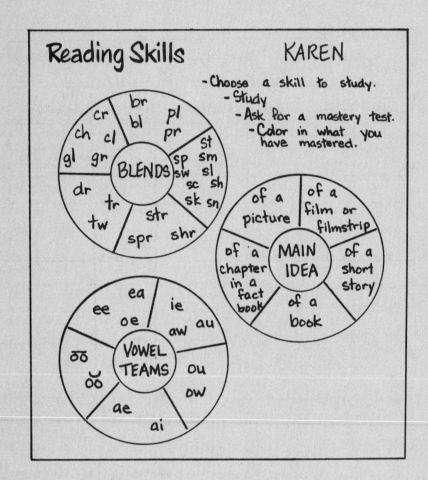

I KNOW...					
the basic addition facts					
the basic subtraction facts					
the basic multiplication facts					
the basic division facts					
I CAN...					
add without regrouping					
add with regrouping					
add columns of numbers					
subtract without regrouping					
subtract with regrouping					

RECORD KEEPING FOR MATH

Individual Record

Each child has a card. The cards for the class may be kept in a three-ring notebook or in a filebox at the math center, or each child may keep his own in his math folder. The child records the date of the test or conference when mastery of the skill is achieved.

Total Class Record

This chart, showing the dates mastery was achieved in various skills, is kept by the teacher. At a glance, the teacher can see the need for specific skill groups and the children who should be in the group. For example, Mary, Karen, and Tommy might be part of a group to learn addition with regrouping. Both charts can be used to keep records of the computational skills mastered.

	Add without regrouping	Add with regrouping	Column addition	
JOHN A.	9/27	9/30	10/30	
MARY	9/30	10/7		
BETH	9/30		9/30	
STAN D.	9/30	10/30	11/30	
TOMMY	9/30			
KAREN	9/30		10/15	

Apron

The teacher or student writes what the student will be learning on an index card and it is filed in the appropriately labeled pocket of the apron. When the skill is learned, the child moves the card to the other pocket, thereby feeling a sense of accomplishment. This also helps to differentiate what a child needs to learn from what he has already learned. Each child can design his own apron and they can be hung on hangers from a chart rack or classroom clothesline.

Balloon

Each child writes the skill he will be studying on a balloon and colors it yellow. He recolors the balloon with a red crayon when he has mastered the skill. An orange balloon signifies that the child has learned that skill and is ready to tackle a new one.

RECORD KEEPING FOR SPELLING

Spelling Scroll

The student shows that he has learned a spelling word by using it in his monthly story. The scroll keeps track of words learned and shows the student's ability to use words in their proper context. A comparison of monthly stories will provide evidence of the student's progress in spelling and writing.

Spelling Patterns

This record-keeping instrument focuses on the structural rules related to learning how to spell. The teacher fills in the headings after determining the rules which are most appropriate for her class. A check next to a student's name indicates that he has learned to apply the rule.

STUDENTS	short vowels	silent e	endings	double consonants	Suffixes, prefixes			
Paul								
Jean								
Sally L.								
Jerry								

Spelling Assessment Sheet

This instrument helps the teacher determine each student's ability to apply spelling skills, to learn new words, and to use spelling words in written context. The teacher assesses each student according to subjective and objective methods.

Spelling Box

Each pupil maintains a spelling box to keep track of the words he is studying and the words he has learned. The words in the section labeled "Words I Know" can be used as a source for developing a review spelling list. Students can exchange words to form their new spelling lists.

SPELLING / VOCABULARY DEVELOPMENT			
Needs basic words often	Asks for new words	Looks up own words	Attempts to spell phonetically

Name _Dolores_

Date 4-10	Skill being studied periods	Activity	Written work	Mastery

Activity.
Cut and paste   Writing   Mastery

RECORD KEEPING FOR LANGUAGE

Cut and Paste

A student cuts the symbol which indicates his level of progress from the bottom of the page. The symbol is pasted into the appropriate column on the ditto and the activity and date are entered.

Writing Sampler

The teacher and the student define the skill that needs to be developed from the student's own writing. A sample which shows the deficient skill is cut and pasted onto a page in the sampler. A sample showing the student's progress is later cut and pasted on the same page.

MY Writing Sampler

Date: _2-17-71_
Skill: _even spacing_

1st sample

The magic flower grew until it reached the roof-tops

Improved sample

The rocket ship had a silvery, shiny look. It was

Language Study Box

The teacher surveys basic curriculum or class interests and abilities to determine the language areas to be emphasized. These areas become headings for the dividers in the record-keeping box. Each child has a card or cards which identifies his learning need(s) and his progress. The card(s) are filed behind the subject area in which he is working.

My Writing Book

Each student has his own writing book which contains all of his writings. It helps the teacher and student to diagnose the student's needs, and is a continuous record of communication between the teacher and the student.

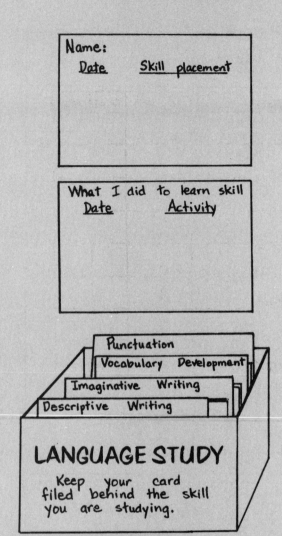

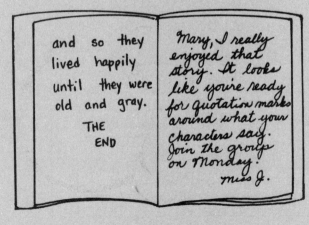

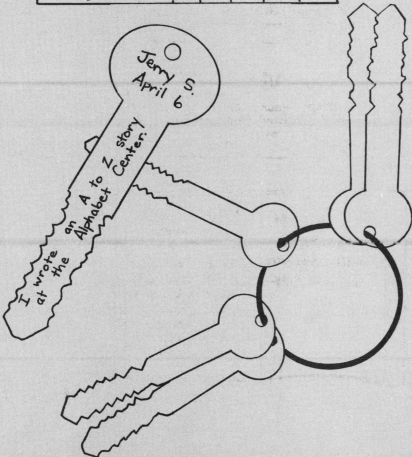

NAME ✓ CHECKING UP ON WHAT I'VE DONE	WEEK OF				
✱ daily "musts"	MON.	TUES.	WED.	THURS.	FRI.
✱ Math Activity					
Independent Study					
Story or poem writing					
✱ Reading					
Handwriting					
Art or Music					
✱ Measurement or Cooking Center					
Animal Stories or Magnets Center					

RECORD KEEPING FOR THE WHOLE DAY

Checking Up

Students are required to do the daily musts which have been filled in by the teacher. They complete the rest of their weekly schedule according to their own choices. Students then check off what they have done.

Key Chain

A different colored key is designated for each working area. After working in an area the student fills out a key and adds it to his key chain. In this way he keeps a record of what he did during the day or week. Adding keys to his key chain gives the student a sense of accomplishment and enables the teacher to see how he utilized his time.

Evaluation
7

LOOKING AT LEARNING OUTCOMES

Since the basic purpose of the evaluation process is to enable the student to perceive his progress in relation to his abilities, evaluation itself is more important than the method that is used. The emphasis is on self-evaluation.

"What have you done?" "How well have you done it?" "How do you feel about what you have done?" These are the questions which students are most frequently asked during the evaluation process.

Evaluation must be an integral part of the instructional program and the school day. The teacher's responsibility is to plan the method and time for evaluation and to teach the students how to evaluate. The type of evaluation used is dependent on the student and the learning activity, and may be either oral or written.

Evaluating Academic Growth

The evaluation tool designed for measuring cognitive or academic growth may ask for either a subjective or an objective response. The student's progress may be recorded intermittently or consistently over a period of time.

Evaluating Personal Growth

The basic tool for this type of evaluation is primarily the subjective type which allows the student to express his feelings freely. The student's attitudes about school and his work are included in this affective type of evaluation. Evaluation of the student's self-concept helps him to answer, "Who am I?"

EVALUATION CONFERENCE

The evaluation method which provides the greatest opportunity for student-teacher interaction is the evaluation conference. It is structured to give the student a chance to share his accomplishments and his feelings concerning them. This time is spent in dialogue which allows *both* the teacher and the student to ask and respond to questions and concerns. The student may be asked to demonstrate his newly acquired skills or knowledge. The most beneficial means of evaluating such student progress is to ask the student to apply his learnings in a new or different context. The key to a successful evaluation conference is to provide enough time to *share, discuss,* and *react.* An evaluation conference implies shared leadership and responsibility between the student and the teacher.

Conference Musts

Designating a conference period or block of time
Designing a method for children to sign up for a conference time
Determining a place for the conference
Deciding the standards which other students in the class must follow while the teacher is conferencing
Indicating to the students what is to be brought to the conference
Reminding children to prepare questions they wish to ask.

SELF-EVALUATIONS OF ACADEMIC AND SOCIAL GROWTH

Measuring Up

This self-evaluation tool may be used by the student for assessing any or all learning experiences. A time designated for evaluating reinforces the importance of doing this type of activity.

Diary

Students may keep a diary to record their feelings about a particular learning activity or about the experiences of the entire school day.

How Do I Measure Up?

Date: _____

What I did:

_____
_____
_____
_____

How I felt about what I did:

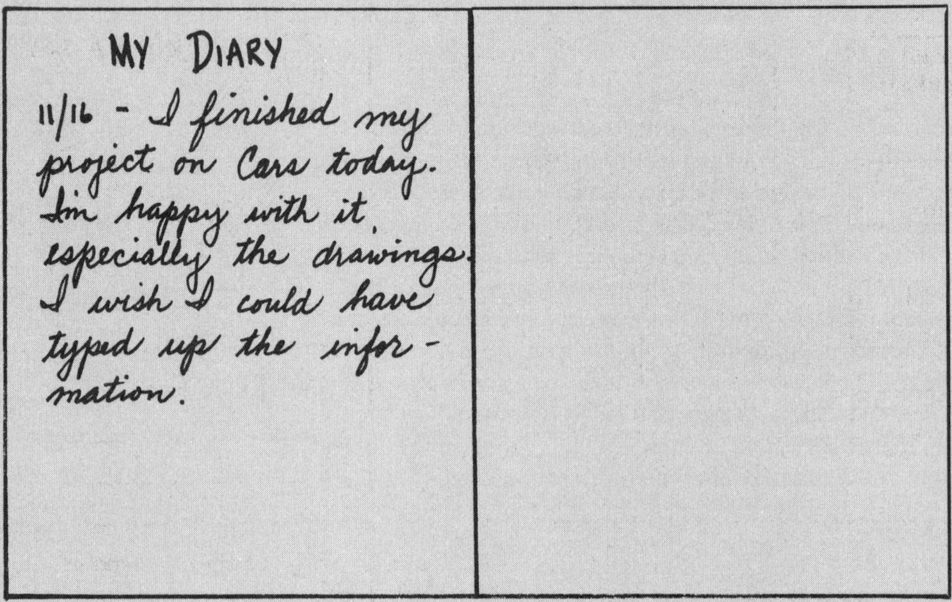

_____
_____
_____
_____
_____

My Diary

11/16 — I finished my project on Cars today. I'm happy with it, especially the drawings. I wish I could have typed up the information.

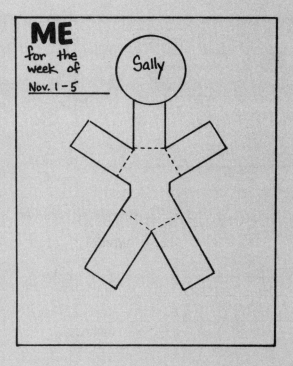

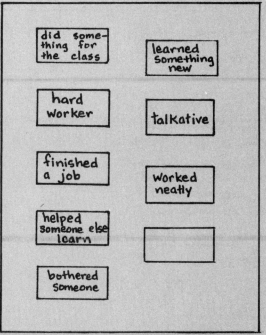

Me

The child draws his face onto the figure. At the close of each school week, he selects the characteristic which best describes him for that week. He cuts and pastes this onto the stick figure. The completed figure provides an accounting of the child's feeling about himself or his work.

Taking a Look at Myself

Effective with older children, this worksheet helps to differentiate the types of goals students can have as they work in the classroom. These goals can be related to a particular learning activity or to a given period of time within the school week. This type of device encourages a student to be responsible for his own learning and behavior.

Continuum

This instrument presents students with examples of behavior. Each behavior is shown with its opposite. Students are to place a mark on the continuum to indicate what they feel their behavior is most like. This can be filled out before and after a given period. In this way the student can compare how he expects to behave with his actual behavior.

Profile

Each child makes a profile of himself. In an individual conference with the teacher, learning or behavioral goals are set for the student. He records these on his profile. After a designated period of time, the student also records his accomplishments.

Worksheets

CONTENTS

BE A GOOD GARDENER

Grow the flowers in ABC order in the flower pot.

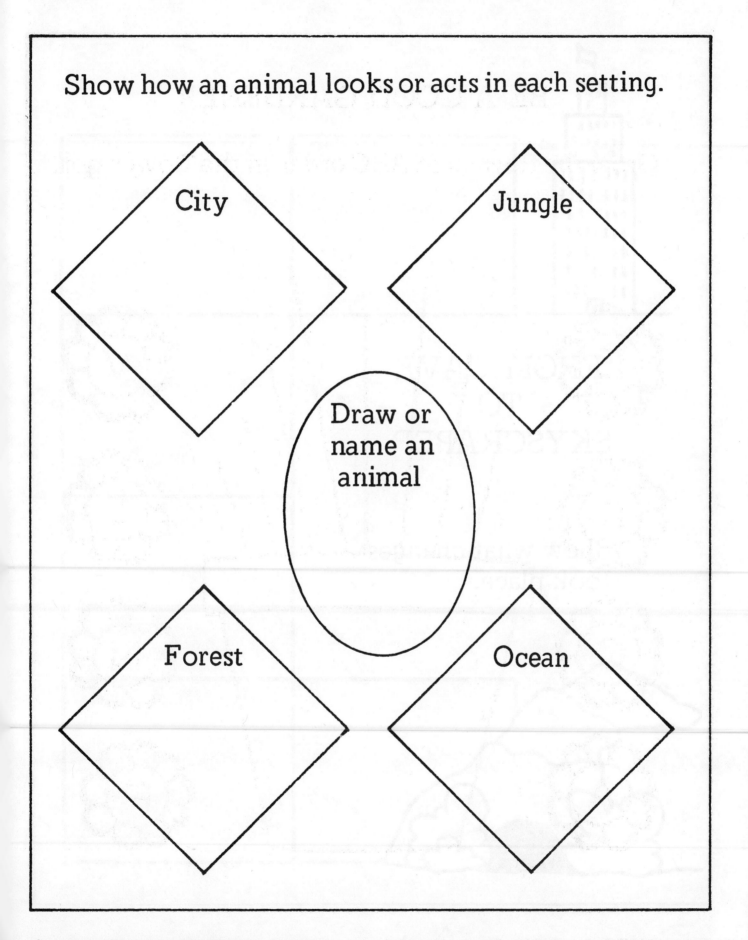

Show how an animal looks or acts in each setting.

City

Jungle

Draw or
name an
animal

Forest

Ocean

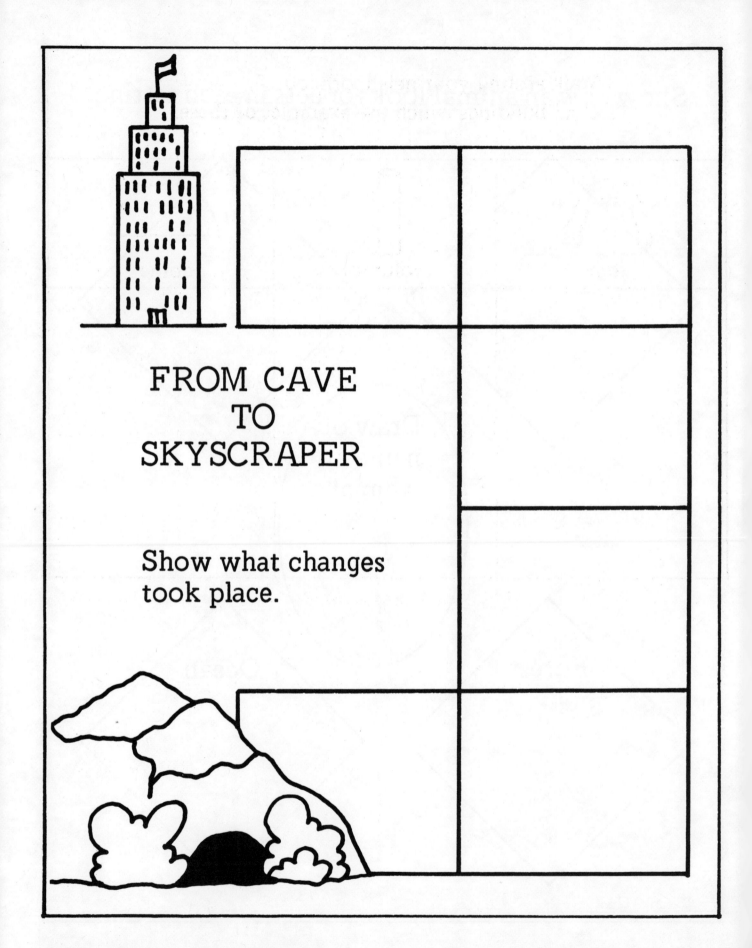

FROM CAVE
TO
SKYSCRAPER

Show what changes
took place.

Walk around your neighborhood.
Find buildings which use examples of these:

arch	column	dome

Choose a painting in one of these styles. Draw it in its correct frame. Change it to show how it would look in one or both of the other styles.

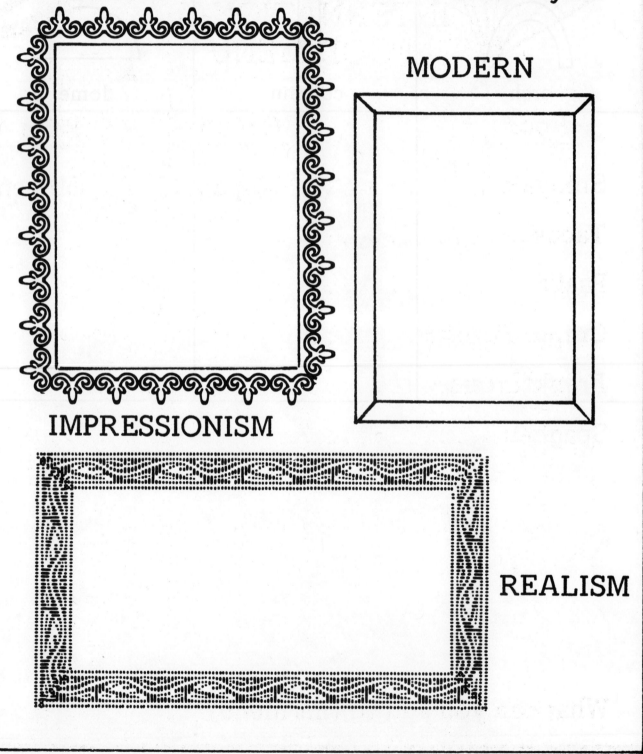

MODERN

IMPRESSIONISM

REALISM

INTERNATIONAL FOOD MENU

Food	Country	Price
Sukiyaki	Japan	50 yen
Tacos		
Paella		
Crepes Suzette		
Frankfurters		
Spaghetti		

What can you add to this menu?

What foods are made in these ways?

on the stove

in the freezer

in the refrigerator

in the oven

in the broiler

no cooking needed

on the barbeque

in a special appliance

Design a new house from those around you. Choose each feature from a different house in your neighborhood.

Design a Home

Features you may wish to include:

door	walkway	steps
porch	T.V. antenna	chimney
mail box	and ? ? ?	

ALIKE > and < DIFFERENT

Choose 6 houses on a block. Use words or drawings to compare a feature of the houses, such as T.V. antennas, doors, windows or shrubbery. Look for things that are alike and different.

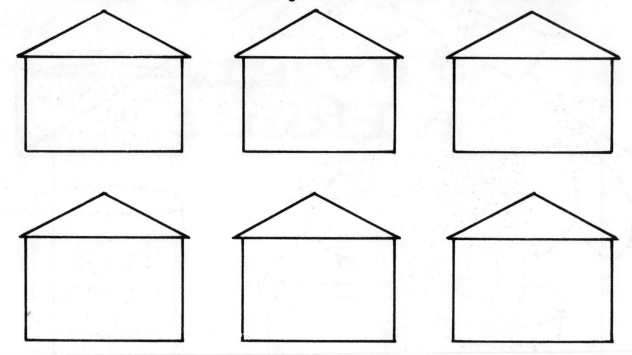

Color in the ingredients you would add to a fairy tale.

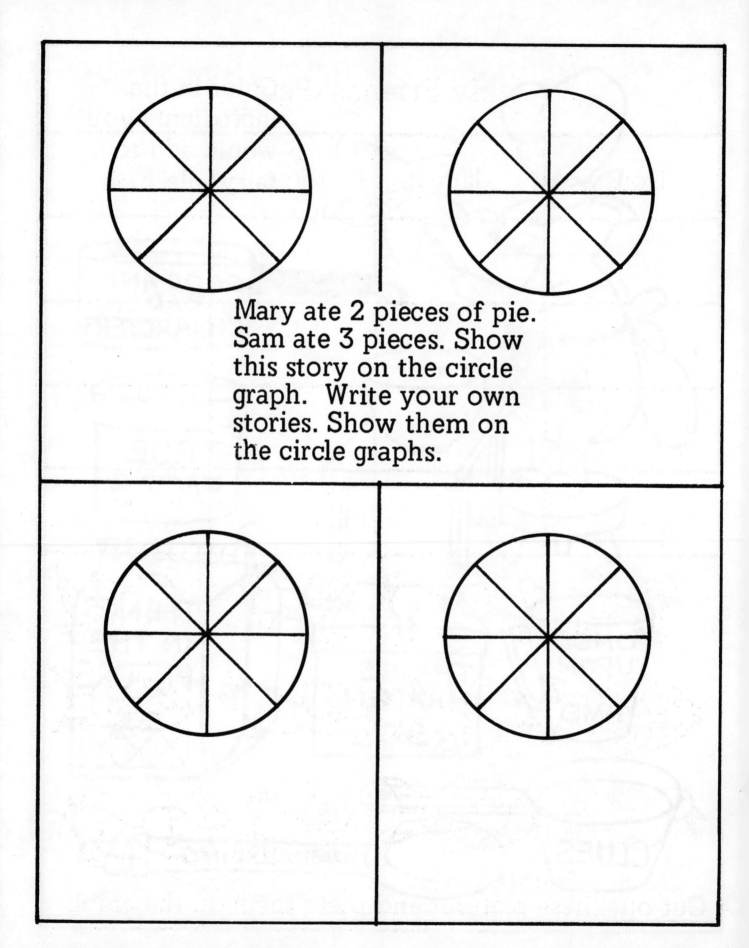

Mary ate 2 pieces of pie. Sam ate 3 pieces. Show this story on the circle graph. Write your own stories. Show them on the circle graphs.

My Friends' Pets

Dogs	Cats	Birds	Fish

Cut out these pictures and paste them on the graph.

TRACE—PRACTICE—PERFECT

1. Choose a letter to practice.
2. Have the teacher write it for you.
3. Trace the letter as many times as you need to.

Trace	Practice	Write your perfect letter

Practice: your name
            or
            a word
            or
            a letter

Make it into a cartoon character.

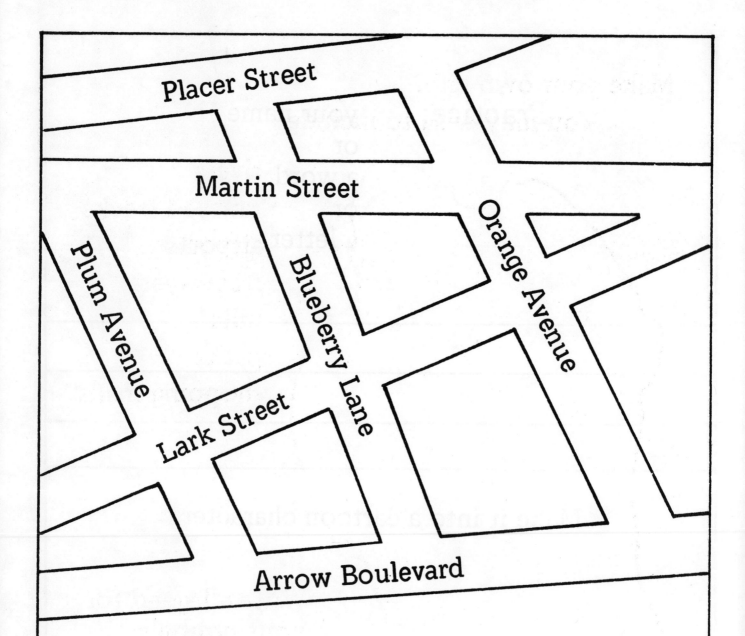

Map a route for an underground transit system using these streets.

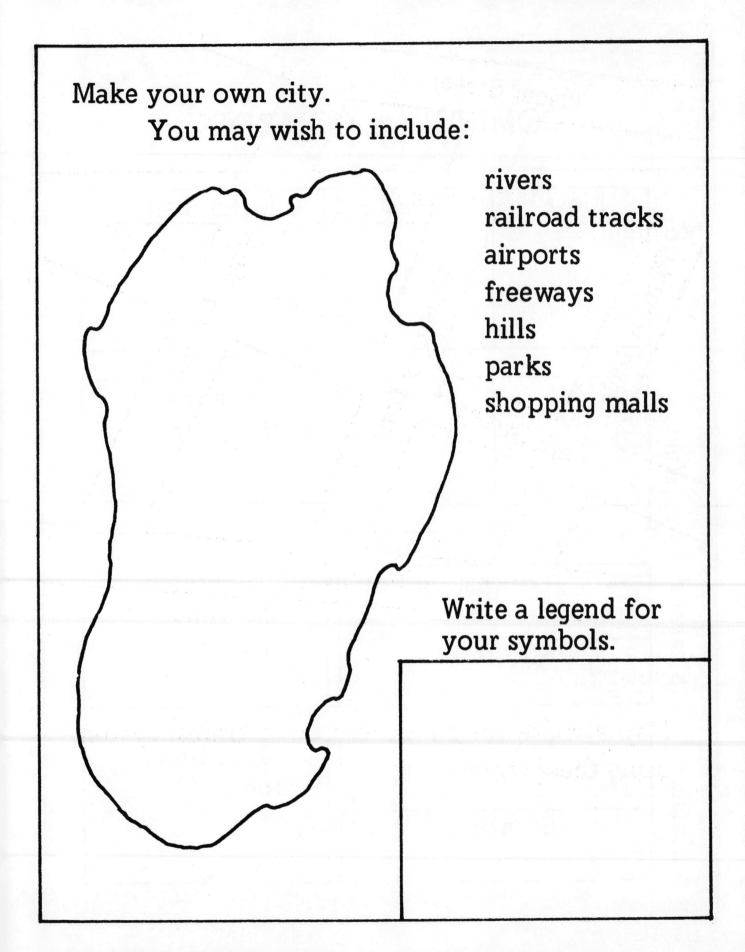

Make your own city.
    You may wish to include:

rivers
railroad tracks
airports
freeways
hills
parks
shopping malls

Write a legend for
your symbols.

COMPARE & COMBINE

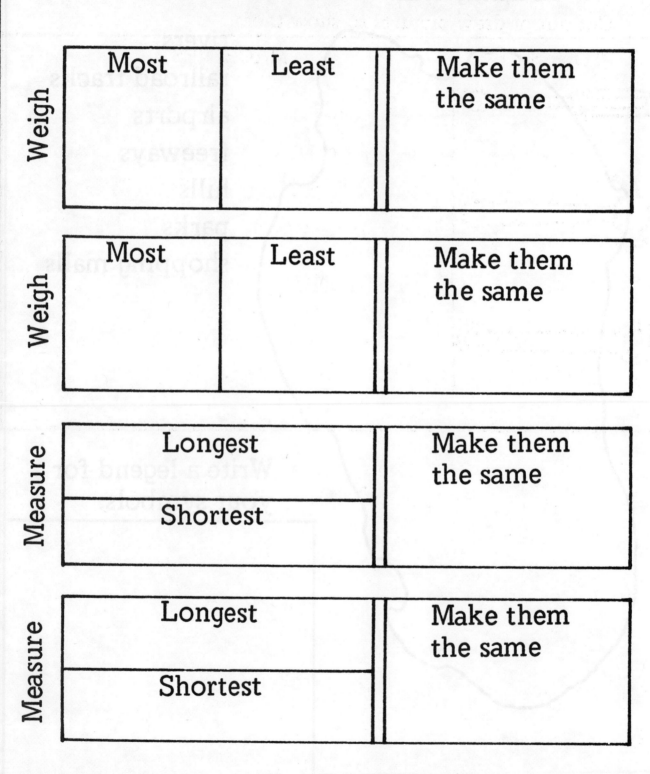

Weigh	Most	Least	Make them the same

Weigh	Most	Least	Make them the same

Measure	Longest	Make them the same
	Shortest	

Measure	Longest	Make them the same
	Shortest	

FIND MACHINES THAT DO THE SAME KIND OF WORK AS THE TOOL

(For example, a screwdriver turns; what machines turn?)
Cut out or draw pictures to show them.

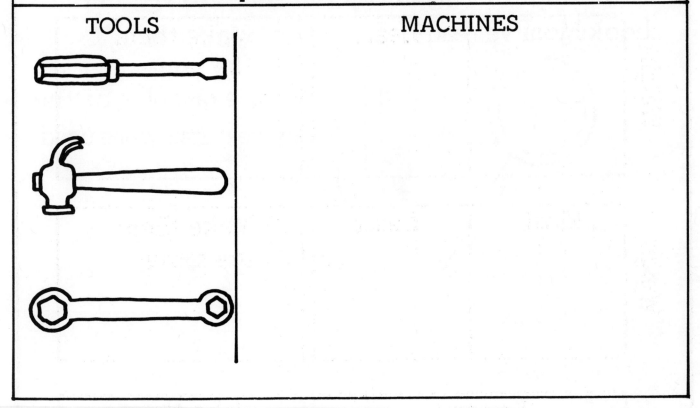

TOOLS   MACHINES

CRIME DETECTION LAB

How were the mysteries or crimes solved in the books you've read?

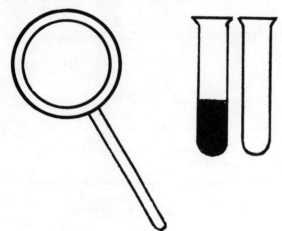

Draw examples of the devices that were used.

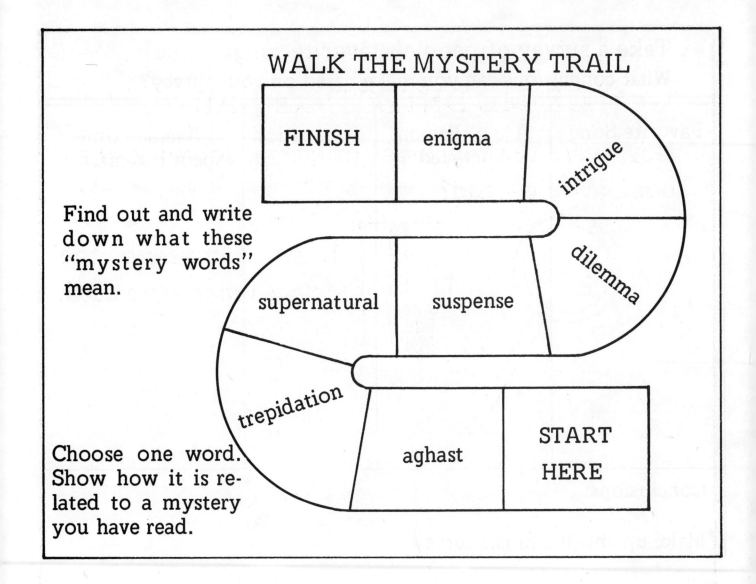

WALK THE MYSTERY TRAIL

FINISH

enigma

intrigue

dilemma

suspense

supernatural

Find out and write down what these "mystery words" mean.

trepidation

aghast

START HERE

Choose one word. Show how it is related to a mystery you have read.

Take a survey of people's favorite songs.
What conclusions can you make based on your survey?

Favorite Song	Age of Person Surveyed	Occupation	Average time spent listening to radio per day

Conclusions:

*Make up another music survey.

Listen to 10 records at home or at school. Write the song titles on one of the record categories below.

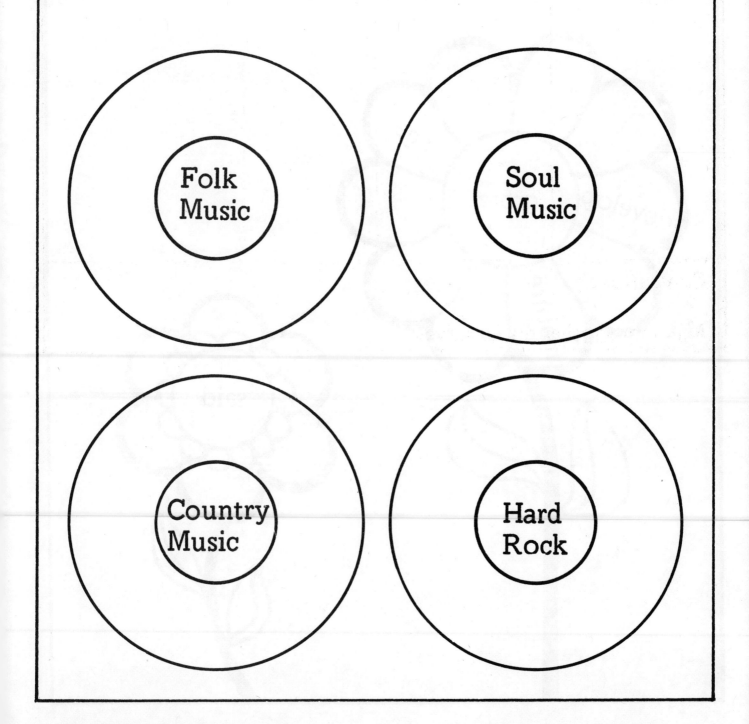

Fill the garden with synonym flowers.
How many can you grow?

Create the course that finishes the story by writing a part of it on each rocket.

Problem: Two space vehicles from different countries are on a "crash" course in space.

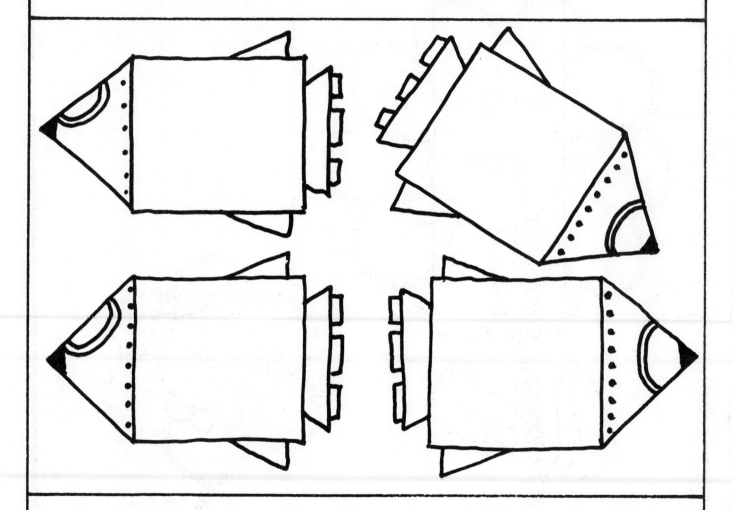

Solution: The Interplanetary Traffic Control Agency felt satisfied with their decision.

MAKE A SEQUENCE PUZZLE

Draw the main parts of your favorite story in the sections below. Paste this page on cardboard. Cut the sections apart to make a puzzle for others to do. Don't forget to put the answers on the back.

Sub Set Insects

Use the set members on the bodies to write subsets on the insects' legs.

Cut and paste the number that matches each set.

N { 🍎 🍌 🍐 } = ☐

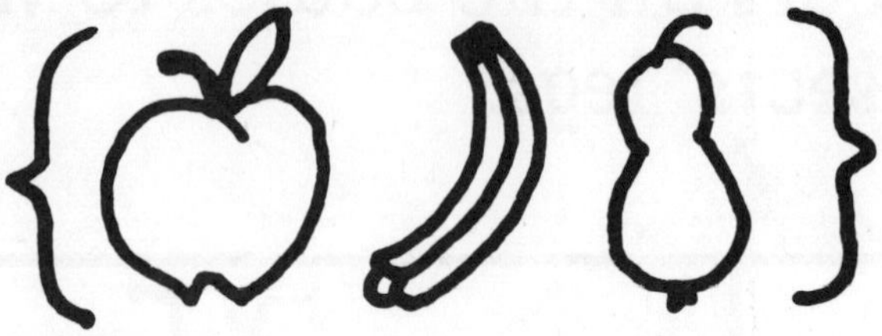

N { 🥛 🍽 🏺 🥄🍴 } = ☐

N { ▱ ▱ } = ☐

N { } = ☐

N { ⚾ ▢ ◇ ○ △ ▯ } = ☐

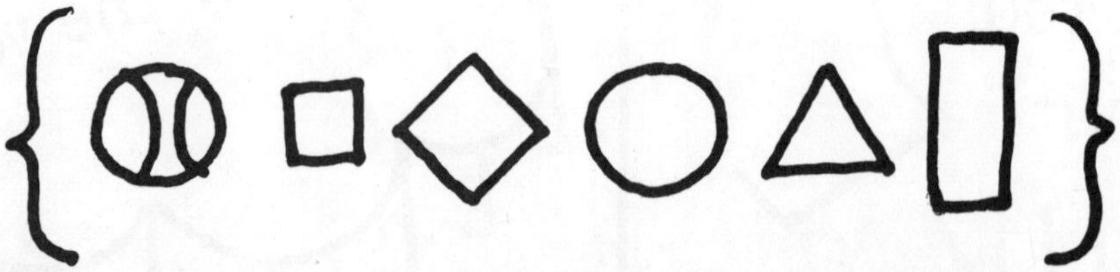

4	6	1	3	0	5		2

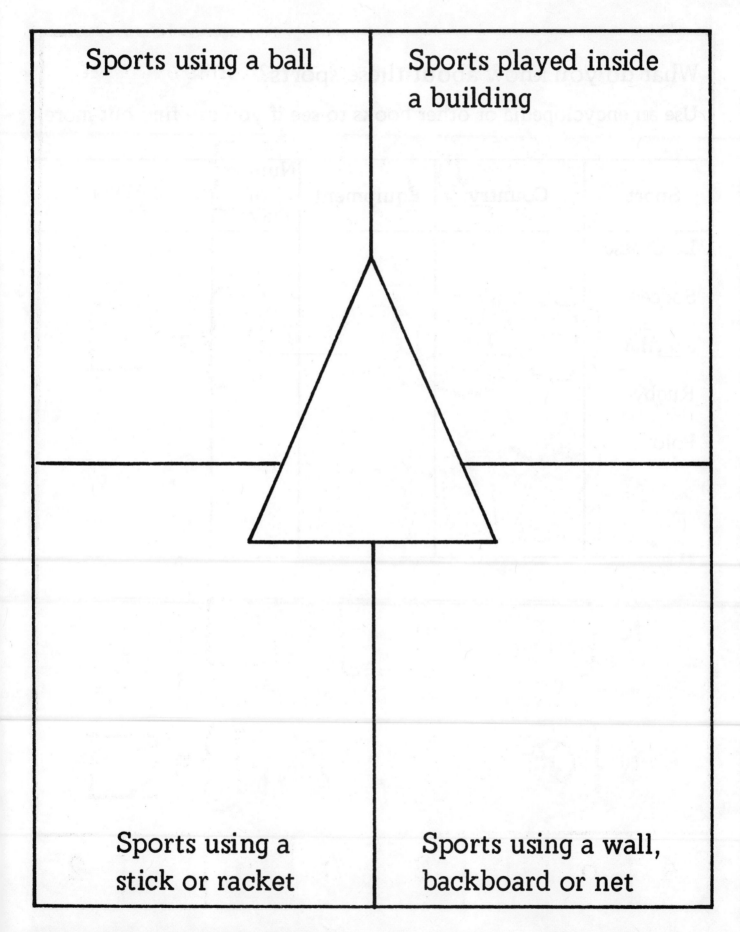

Sports using a ball

Sports played inside
a building

Sports using a
stick or racket

Sports using a wall,
backboard or net

What do you know about these sports?

Use an encyclopedia or other books to see if you can find out more.

Sport	Country	Equipment	Number of Players	Playing Area
La Crosse				
Soccer				
Jai Alai				
Rugby				
Polo				

READ A
TALL
TALE

Write the TALL happenings from a TALL TALE on each tree trunk.

DOES THE COMMERCIAL SELL?

Product: _____

Who are they trying to sell to? _____

_____

Do you think it's a good product? _____

Why? _____

_____

Would you buy it? _____

Elements of the commercial

_____ Musical jingle   _____ Slogan

_____ Background music   _____ Humor

_____ Well-known personality

_____ Factual information

_____ Other

Design your own commercial here.

Survey people to find out if they like your commercial.